PIES & TARTS

Consultant Editor:
Valerie Ferguson

southwater

Contents

Introduction

The delicious aroma of pastry, baked to perfection with a succulent filling, is irresistible. Food that is cooked enclosed in pastry seems enhanced as its flavours are "locked in" by the crisp, golden jacket, the pastry absorbing any that might otherwise be lost and so itself becoming even tastier.

Pies and tarts are not difficult to make, as this book demonstrates. Once you have mastered a few basic techniques, you can go on to cook any number of impressive dishes. Here is a collection of scrumptious savoury and sweet pies and tarts, including fish and seafood; poultry, game and meat; vegetarian; fruit; and chocolate and nut. Some are suitable for everyday meals, others for entertaining and special occasions. They range from Tuna Galette, Lamb Pie with Pear & Mint Sauce and Goat's Cheese Pastries to Filo-topped Apple Pie and Chocolate Truffle Tart.

Pastry freezes extremely well, so busy people will find it convenient to make a large batch and freeze it in smaller quantities for later use. However, for those with no time even to do this, ready-made fresh and frozen pastry of various types is available in supermarkets. Why not treat yourself to a delicious home-made pie today!

Types of Pastry

Shortcrust Pastry

One of the easiest and most versatile of pastries, shortcrust consists of flour and fat, with just enough liquid to bind the ingredients together. Always use iced water and, if time permits, wrap shortcrust pastry in clear film and chill it for 30 minutes before rolling it out.

Above: Sweet shortcrust pastry tartlets.

Rich or Sweet Shortcrust Pastry

Rich pastry sets to a crisper crust than plain shortcrust. It is often used for fruit pies. Use the shortcrust recipe but use butter and substitute an egg yolk for part of the liquid. For a sweet pastry, add 30–45 ml/2–3 tbsp caster sugar after rubbing in the fat.

Puff Pastry

This is made in such a way that it separates into crisp layers when cooked, thanks to the air trapped in it. A block of butter is wrapped in a basic dough, the pastry is then turned, rolled, folded and chilled several times. If using frozen puff pastry, thaw slowly.

Rough Puff Pastry

Diced fat is mixed with the flour but not rubbed in, so the fat can be seen in the dough. The pastry is rolled and folded several times before being rested and baked. The fat used should be very cold and it helps if the flour is chilled.

Choux Pastry

The butter is melted with water and then the flour added all at once and vigorously beaten in before the eggs are added. It is easy to make, but must be carefully measured.

Filo Pastry

This Greek pastry comes in paper-thin sheets, which are layered, then cooked until crisp. Each layer must be brushed with oil or melted butter, and any spare pastry should be covered with a clean, damp dish towel.

Flaky Pastry

This involves making a dough with half the stipulated amount of butter, then softening the rest to the same consistency as the dough and dotting it over the surface of the rolled-out pastry, which is folded, turned, rolled and chilled several times. When baked, it separates into light, crisp leaves.

Hot Water Crust Pastry

Hot liquid is added to the dry ingredients and the pastry is kept warm while resting. It is most traditionally used for raised pies.

Techniques

Rubbing In

Add the diced fat to the flour. Using the fingertips and thumbs, draw up a small amount of mixture and rub together to break it down into crumbs. Repeat the process lifting the mixture each time to incorporate air, until no large lumps of fat remain. Do not overwork the dough.

Using a Pastry Blender

A pastry blender is a gadget comprising between five and eight arched wires on a wooden handle. Some cooks prefer it for rubbing in as it stops warm hands softening the fat, but it can break down the fat almost too efficiently. Use the blender for half the fat, and add the rest in pea–size pieces.

Rolling Out

A smooth layer of pastry that will not distort or shrink in baking is the desired result. The key to successful rolling out is to handle the dough gently.

1 Using an even pressure, roll out the dough on a lightly floured surface. Start in the centre of the dough and roll out towards the edge.

2 Give the dough a quarter turn from time to time during the rolling, so that it rolls out evenly and does not stick to the surface. Continue the rolling out process until the dough circle is about 5 cm/2 in larger than the size of the tin. It should be about 3 mm/ ⅛ in thick.

Lining a Tin

Set the rolling pin on the dough, near one side. Fold the outside edge over the pin, then roll the pin to wrap the dough around it. Hold over the tin and unroll the dough into the tin. Lift and ease the dough into the tin, gently pressing the base and side. Turn excess dough over the rim and trim it with a knife or scissors.

Glazing

For a rich, golden crust, brush the pastry with beaten egg, a mixture of beaten egg and water, or milk just before baking. For a sweet pie, you can add a light dusting of caster sugar on top of the glaze.

Crimping a Pastry Shell

Make a "V" with the thumb and forefinger of one hand, pressing lightly on the pastry. Then use the index finger of your other hand to push between the "V" inwards. Or press the knuckle of one hand against the inner edge, using the other hand to pinch around your finger.

Baking Blind

This refers to the method of partially or fully baking an unfilled pastry case. Line it with greaseproof paper and add an even layer of baking beans (use dried beans kept for the purpose or special china beans). Bake the case for 10 minutes, then remove the paper and baking beans and return the pastry case to the oven for 5 minutes more, or longer if it is not to be cooked again after fi'ling.

Making Shortcrust Pastry

Use half butter or margarine and half white vegetable fat, or all the same fat.

Lines a 23 cm/9 in pastry case

INGREDIENTS
225 g/8 oz/2 cups plain white flour
1.5 ml/¼ tsp salt
115 g/4 oz/½ cup fat, chilled and diced
45–60 ml/3–4 tbsp iced water

1 Sift the flour and salt into a bowl, raising the sieve to incorporate as much air as possible. Add the fat. Rub into the flour until the mixture resembles breadcrumbs.

2 Sprinkle 45 ml/3 tbsp water over. Toss the mixture with your fingers to combine and moisten.

3 Press the dough into a ball. If it is too dry, add the remaining water.

4 Shape the ball of dough into an oblong or oval then wrap in clear film and allow to chill in the fridge for 30 minutes before using.

Making Puff Pastry

Puff pastry has a feather–light texture because of its high butter content.

Makes 500 g/1¼ lb

INGREDIENTS
200 g//7 oz/⅞ cup cold unsalted butter
200 g//7 oz/1½ cups fine plain flour
1.5 ml/l¼ tsp salt
125 ml/4 fl oz/½ cup cold water

1 Cut the butter into 14 pieces and place in the freezer for 30 minutes.

2 Put the flour and salt in a food processor and pulse to combine. Add the butter and pulse three times; there should still be large lumps of butter. Run the machine for 5 seconds while pouring the water through the feed tube, then stop the machine. The dough should look curdy.

3 Tip the mixture on to a lightly floured, cool work surface and gather into a flat ball. If the visible butter is soft, chill the dough for 30 minutes.

4 Roll out the dough on a floured surface to a 40 x 25 cm/16 x 6 in rectangle. Fold in thirds, bringing one end down to cover the middle, then fold the other end over it, like folding a letter. Roll out again to a rectangle and fold again the same way. Chill for 30 minutes. Roll and fold twice more then chill, wrapped for 30 minutes.

Tuna Galette

This flaky pastry tart combines soft-centred eggs and a slightly piquant fish filling. It makes a wonderful dish for a summer supper and is also a great buffet-table standby.

Serves 4

INGREDIENTS
2 sheets ready-rolled puff pastry
beaten egg, to glaze
60 ml/4 tbsp olive oil
175 g/6 oz tuna steak
2 onions, sliced
1 large red pepper, seeded
   and chopped
2 garlic cloves, crushed
45 ml/3 tbsp capers, drained
5 ml/1 tsp grated lemon rind
30 ml/2 tbsp lemon juice
4 eggs
salt and freshly ground black pepper
30 ml/2 tbsp chopped fresh flat leaf parsley,
   to garnish

1 Preheat the oven to 190°C/375°F/ Gas 5. Lay one sheet of pastry on a floured baking sheet and cut to a 28 x 18 cm/11 x 7 in rectangle. Brush the whole sheet with beaten egg.

COOK'S TIPS: If using fresh, unfrozen pastry, the remaining pastry can be wrapped in clear film and frozen. Allow to defrost at room temperature for 1 hour before using. To make sure the eggs do not become hard during baking, cover the tart with lightly oiled foil.

2 Cut the second sheet of pastry to the same size. Cut out a rectangle from the centre and discard, leaving a 2.5 cm/1 in border. Carefully lift the border on to the first sheet.

3 Brush the border with beaten egg and prick the base. Bake for about 15 minutes until golden and well risen.

4 Heat 30 ml/2 tbsp of the oil in a frying pan and fry the tuna steak for 2–3 minutes on each side until golden but still pale pink in the middle. Transfer the tuna to a plate and flake into small pieces.

5 Add the remaining oil to the pan and fry the onions, red pepper and garlic for 6–8 minutes until softened, stirring occasionally. Remove the pan from the heat and stir in the tuna, capers and lemon rind and juice. Season well with salt and freshly ground black pepper.

6 Spoon the filling into the prepared pastry case and level the surface with the back of a large spoon. Carefully break the eggs into the filling and return the galette to the oven for about 10 minutes or until the eggs have just cooked through. Garnish with chopped fresh parsley and serve at once.

Salmon Kulebyaka

A Russian festive dish in which a layer of moist salmon and eggs sits on a bed of buttery, dill-flavoured rice, all encased in crisp puff pastry.

Serves 4

INGREDIENTS
50 g/2 oz/4 tbsp butter
1 small onion, finely chopped
150 g/6 oz/1 cup cooked
    long grain rice
15 ml/1 tbsp chopped fresh dill
15 ml/1 tbsp lemon juice
450 g/1 lb puff pastry, defrosted
    if frozen
450 g/1 lb salmon fillet, skinned and cut
    into 5 cm/2 in pieces
2 eggs, hard-boiled and chopped
beaten egg, to glaze
salt and freshly ground
    black pepper
watercress, to garnish

1 Preheat the oven to 200°C/400°F/ Gas 6. Melt the butter in a medium pan, add the chopped onion and cook gently for 10 minutes or until soft and translucent. Stir in the cooked rice, fresh dill, lemon juice, salt and freshly ground black pepper.

2 Roll out the puff pastry on a lightly floured surface to a 30 cm/12 in square. Spoon the rice mixture over half the pastry, leaving a 1 cm/½ in border around the edges.

3 Arrange the salmon on top, then scatter the chopped eggs over the salmon. Brush the pastry edges with egg, then fold over the filling to make a rectangle, pressing down the edges firmly to seal.

4 Carefully lift the pastry on to a lightly oiled baking sheet. Glaze with beaten egg, then pierce the pastry a few times with a skewer to make holes for the steam to escape.

5 Bake on the middle shelf of the oven for 40 minutes, covering with foil after about 30 minutes to prevent the pastry burning. Leave to cool on the baking sheet, before cutting into slices. Garnish with sprigs of watercress and serve.

Smoked Salmon Quiche with Potato Pastry

The ingredients in this light but richly flavoured quiche perfectly complement the melt-in-the-mouth pastry made with potatoes.

Serves 6

INGREDIENTS
115 g/4 oz floury maincrop potatoes, diced
225 g/8 oz/2 cups plain flour, sifted
115 g/4 oz/½ cup butter, diced
½ egg, beaten
10 ml/2 tsp chilled water

FOR THE FILLING
275 g/10 oz smoked salmon
6 eggs, beaten
150 ml/¼ pint/⅔ cup full-fat milk
300 ml/½ pint/1¼ cups double cream
30–45 ml/2–3 tbsp chopped fresh dill, plus
    extra to garnish
30 ml/2 tbsp capers, drained and chopped
salt and freshly ground black pepper

1 Boil the potatoes in a large saucepan of lightly salted water for 15 minutes or until tender. Drain well through a colander and return to the pan. Mash the potatoes until smooth and set aside to cool completely.

COOK'S TIPS: To ensure the base cooks through it is vital to preheat a baking sheet in the oven first. Make the most of smoked salmon offcuts for this quiche, as they will work out much cheaper.

2 Place the flour in a bowl and rub in the butter to form fine crumbs. Beat in the potatoes and egg. Bring the mixture together, adding chilled water if needed, to make a dough.

3 Roll out the pastry on a lightly floured surface and use to line a deep, 23 cm/9 in, round, loose-based, fluted flan tin. Chill for 1 hour.

4 Preheat the oven to 200°C/400°F/ Gas 6. Heat a baking sheet in the oven. To make the filling, chop the salmon into bite-size pieces and set aside.

5 In a bowl, beat the eggs, milk and cream. Stir in the dill, capers and black pepper. Gently stir in the salmon.

6 Prick the pastry case and pour in the mixture. Bake on the baking sheet for 35–45 minutes until set and golden. Serve warm, garnished with chopped dill.

Onion & Anchovy Tart

Sweet, slowly cooked onions in a crisp, egg-enriched pastry case.

Serves 8

INGREDIENTS
150 g/5 oz/1¼ cups flour
2.5 ml/½ tsp salt
115 g/4 oz/½ cup chilled butter, cut into pieces
1 egg yolk
30–45 ml/2–3 tbsp iced water

FOR THE FILLING
60 ml/4 tbsp olive oil
900 g/2 lb onions, sliced
5 ml/1 tsp dried thyme
2–3 tomatoes, sliced
24 small black olives, pitted
50 g/2 oz can anchovy fillets, drained
 and sliced
6 sun-dried tomatoes, cut into slivers
salt and freshly ground black pepper
fresh flat leaf parsley sprigs, to garnish

1 Sift the flour and salt into a bowl. Cut in the butter to resemble coarse crumbs. Stir in the egg yolk and enough water to make a soft dough. Roll out 3 mm/⅛ in thick on a lightly floured surface. Transfer to a 23 cm/9 in tart tin and trim. Chill for 30 minutes.

2 Heat the oil in a frying pan. Add the onion, thyme and seasoning. Cook over low heat, covered, for 25 minutes. Uncover and cook until soft, then cool. Preheat the oven to 200°C/400°F/Gas 6.

3 Spoon the onions into the pastry case and arrange the remaining filling ingredients in a lattice pattern. Bake for 20–25 minutes until golden. Serve warm or cold, garnished with parsley.

Seafood Surprise

The simple filling in this seafood dish makes for easy preparation.

Serves 6

INGREDIENTS
175 g/6 oz cooked peeled prawns
150 g/5 oz/⅔ cup soft cheese with herbs
  and garlic
15 ml/1 tbsp chopped fresh tarragon
  (optional)
175 g/6 oz can crab meat, drained
225 g/8 oz puff pastry, defrosted if frozen
8 small or 4 large trout fillets, skinned
salt and freshly ground black pepper
beaten egg, to glaze
fresh tarragon sprig, to garnish

1 Preheat the oven to 220°C/425°F/ Gas 7. Grease a baking sheet. Mix the prawns with the cheese, tarragon, if using, and crab meat.

2 Cut the pastry in two portions, one slightly larger. Roll the smaller into an oblong 30 x 13 cm/12 x 5 in. Place on the baking sheet. Top with the trout, leaving a border, and season. Top with prawn mixture. Roll the remaining pastry slightly larger, fold in half lengthways, then make cuts into the folded edge two-thirds of the way across. Stop 5 cm/2 in from each end and cut every 1.5 cm/½ in.

3 Brush the border with beaten egg, then cover the filling with the unfolded pastry, pressing the edges. Brush with egg. Bake for 15 minutes, then for 15–20 minutes at 200°C/ 400°F/Gas 6. Garnish with tarragon and serve.

Chicken Pie with Mushrooms

The filling in this pie has an intense mushroom flavour, using chicken stock rather than the more usual milk and butter.

Serves 4–6

INGREDIENTS
150 g/5 oz/10 tbsp butter or
    margarine, chilled
225 g/8 oz/2 cups plain flour
1 egg yolk
60 ml/4 tbsp cold water

FOR THE FILLING
900 g/2 lb cooked roast or boiled chicken
45 ml/3 tbsp olive oil
275 g/10 oz mixed dark mushrooms
    (flat, oyster or chestnut)
25 ml/1½ tbsp flour
300 ml/½ pint/1¼ cups chicken stock
15 ml/1 tbsp soy sauce
1 egg white, lightly whisked
salt and freshly ground black pepper

1 Cut the butter or margarine into small pieces and then rub it into the flour until the mixture resembles breadcrumbs. Combine the egg yolk with the water and stir into the flour mixture to form a soft dough. Roll into a ball, cover and chill the dough for about 30 minutes.

COOK'S TIP: The pie can be made in advance up to step 4 and chilled overnight or frozen. To cook from frozen, leave at room temperature for a few hours and cook as above.

2 Preheat the oven to 220°C/425°F/ Gas 7. To make the filling, cut the chicken into pieces and place in a greased pie dish of about 1.75 litres/ 3 pints/7½ cups capacity.

3 Heat half the oil in a frying pan. Slice the mushrooms thickly and then sauté them over high heat for about 3 minutes. Add the rest of the oil and stir in the flour. Season with pepper and slowly add the stock, stirring to make a thick sauce.

4 Stir in the soy sauce. Taste and adjust the seasoning as necessary. Pour the mushroom sauce over the chicken.

5 On a floured surface, roll out the pastry. Cut a piece slightly larger than the dish. Cut strips about 2 cm/¾ in wide and place round the rim. Lay the lid on top, pressing down the edges. Trim, mark the edges with the back of a knife and cut slashes in the top. Brush with egg white and bake for 30–35 minutes until golden. Serve.

Chicken en Croûte

Chicken breasts, layered with herb- and orange-flavoured stuffing and wrapped in light puff pastry, make an impressive dinner party dish.

Serves 8

INGREDIENTS
450 g/1 lb puff pastry, defrosted if frozen
4 large boned and skinned chicken breasts
1 egg, beaten
cooked vegetables, to serve

FOR THE STUFFING
115 g/4 oz leeks, thinly sliced
50 g/2 oz streaky bacon, chopped
25 g/1 oz/2 tbsp butter
115 g/4 oz/2 cups fresh white breadcrumbs
30 ml/2 tbsp chopped fresh herbs, e.g.
   parsley, thyme, marjoram and chives
grated rind and juice of 1 large orange
1 egg, beaten
salt and freshly ground black pepper

1 To make the stuffing, cook the leeks and bacon in the butter until soft. Put the breadcrumbs into a bowl with the herbs and seasoning. Add the leeks, bacon and orange rind and bind with egg. If the mixture is too crumbly, add a little orange juice.

2 Preheat the oven to 200°C/400°F/ Gas 6. On a lightly floured surface, roll out the pastry to a rectangle 30 x 40 cm/12 x 16 in. Trim the edges and reserve for the decoration.

3 Place the chicken breasts between two pieces of clear film and flatten to a thickness of 5 mm/¼ in with a rolling pin. Spread one-third of the stuffing over the centre of the pastry. Lay two chicken breasts side by side over the stuffing. Cover with another third of the stuffing, then repeat with the two remaining chicken breasts and the rest of the stuffing.

4 Make a cut diagonally from each corner of the pastry to the chicken. Brush the pastry with beaten egg.

5 Bring up the sides and overlap them slightly. Trim away any excess pastry before folding the ends over like a parcel. Place on a greased baking tray, with the joins underneath.

6 With a sharp knife, lightly criss-cross the pastry into a diamond pattern. Brush with beaten egg. Cut leaves from the trimmings to decorate the top. Bake for 50 minutes–1 hour or until well risen and golden brown on top. Serve with cooked vegetables.

Game Pie with Port

A good game pie is one of the triumphs of traditional British cooking, and this is one of the best. Cut the hot water crust to reveal a rich filling, flavoured with port and juniper berries.

Serves 8–10

INGREDIENTS
450 g/1 lb/4 cups plain flour
10 ml/2 tsp salt
175 g/6 oz/¾ cup lard or white vegetable fat
175 ml/6 fl oz/¾ cup milk, or milk and water
beaten egg, to glaze
10 ml/2 tsp powdered gelatine
30 ml/2 tbsp cold water
salt and freshly ground black pepper
mixed salad, to serve

FOR THE FILLING
675 g/1½ lb lean boneless game, such
   as pheasant, grouse, partridge and
   rabbit, diced
115 g/4 oz rindless streaky bacon
   rashers, chopped
115 g/4 oz minced pork
30 ml/2 tbsp port
10 ml/2 tsp grated orange rind
2 juniper berries, crushed
2.5 ml/½ tsp dried sage

1 Preheat the oven to 200°C/400°F/ Gas 6. Grease a 20 cm/8 in springform cake tin. Sift the flour and salt into a bowl and make a well in the centre.

> COOK'S TIP: Make an extra pastry shape to cover the hole after pouring in the gelatine.

2 In a saucepan, melt the lard or vegetable fat in the milk or milk and water. Bring to the boil, pour into the well in the flour and mix with a wooden spoon until cool enough to handle. Knead to a smooth dough, then wrap in clear film and leave to cool.

3 To make the filling, mix the game, bacon and pork in a bowl. Add the port, orange rind, juniper berries and sage. Season well.

4 Roll out two-thirds of the dough and fit it into the tin, taking care not to stretch it. Do not trim the edge.

5 Fill the pastry case with the meat mixture and smooth the surface. Brush the edge of the pastry with beaten egg. Roll the remaining pastry into a round to fit the top of the pie. Make a hole in the middle for pouring in the gelatine later. Fit the lid in place and seal, trim and crimp the edge.

6 Brush the pastry lid with beaten egg. Decorate the lid with pastry shapes cut from the trimmings and brush them with beaten egg.

7 Bake the pie for 30 minutes, then lower the oven temperature to 180°C/ 350°F/Gas 4 and bake for 1¼ hours, covering the pie with foil if the pastry starts to over-brown.

8 About 20 minutes before the end of the cooking time, remove the sides from the tin. Quickly brush the sides of the pie with egg and return to the oven.

9 Sprinkle the gelatine over the water in a heatproof bowl. When spongy, stir over simmering water until dissolved. Pour through a funnel into the pie and leave to cool. Serve with salad.

Guinness, Beef & Oyster Pie

Layers of crisp puff pastry encase a tasty rich stew of tender beef and fresh oysters: a traditional combination.

Serves 4

INGREDIENTS
450 g/1 lb stewing or braising steak
25 g/1 oz/2 tbsp plain flour
15 ml/1 tbsp vegetable oil
25 g/1 oz/2 tbsp butter
1 onion, sliced
150 ml/¼ pint/⅔ cup Guinness
150 ml/¼ pint/⅔ cup beef stock
5 ml/1 tsp sugar
1 bouquet garni
12 oysters, opened
350 g/12 oz puff pastry, defrosted
    if frozen
1 egg, beaten
salt and freshly ground black pepper
chopped fresh parsley,
    to garnish

1 Preheat the oven to 180°C/350°F/Gas 4. Trim any excess fat from the meat and cut into 2.5 cm/1 in cubes. Place in a bag with the flour and plenty of seasoning. Shake until the meat is well coated.

2 Heat the oil and butter in a flameproof casserole and fry the meat for 10 minutes until well sealed and browned all over. Add the onion and continue cooking for 2–3 minutes until just softened.

3 Pour in the Guinness and stock. Add the sugar and bouquet garni. Cover the casserole and cook in the oven for 1¼ hours.

4 Spoon the stew into a pie dish of about 1.2 litres/2 pints/5 cups capacity discarding the bouquet garni, and leave to cool slightly. Increase the oven temperature to 200°C/400°F/Gas 6.

5 Meanwhile, remove the oysters from their shells and wash. Dry on kitchen paper and stir into the steak and Guinness.

6 On a lightly floured surface, roll out the pastry large enough to fit the pie dish. Brush the edge of the dish with beaten egg and lay the pastry over the top. Trim neatly, decorate and brush with the remaining egg. Bake for 25 minutes until puffed and golden. Serve hot, garnished with parsley.

Lamb Pie with Pear & Mint Sauce

A fruity stuffing nestles inside this lamb, which in turn is wrapped in filo pastry, baked and served with a refreshing sauce.

Serves 6

INGREDIENTS
1 boned mid-loin of lamb, about
  1 kg/2¼ lb after boning
8 large sheets filo pastry
25 g/1 oz/2 tbsp butter
10 ml/2 tsp finely chopped
  fresh mint
fresh flat leaf parsley, to garnish
salt and freshly ground
  black pepper

FOR THE STUFFING
15 g/½ oz/1 tbsp butter
1 small onion, chopped
115 g/4 oz/2 cups
  wholemeal breadcrumbs
grated rind of 1 lemon
400 g/14 oz can pears
1.5 ml/¼ tsp ground ginger
1 small egg, beaten

1 Preheat the oven to 180°C/350°F/ Gas 4. To make the stuffing, melt the butter in a pan, add the onion and cook until soft.

2 Transfer to a mixing bowl and add the breadcrumbs, lemon rind, 175 g/6 oz of the drained pears and the ginger. Season lightly and add enough beaten egg to bind.

3 Spread the lamb out flat, fat side down, and season. Place the stuffing along the middle of the loin and roll carefully, holding with skewers while you sew it together with string. Heat a large roasting tin in the oven and brown the loin slowly on all sides. This will take 20–30 minutes. Leave to cool, then chill until needed.

4 Preheat the oven to 200°C/400°F/ Gas 6. Brush two filo pastry sheets with melted butter. Overlap by about 13 cm/5 in to make a square. Place the next two sheets on top and brush with butter. Continue until all the pastry has been used.

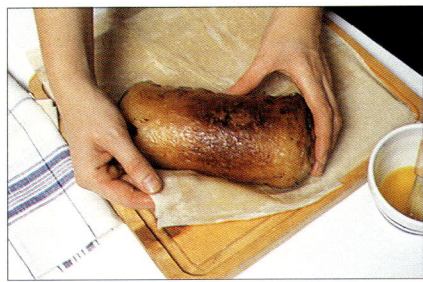

5 Place the roll of lamb diagonally across one corner of the pastry without extending over the sides. Fold the corner over the lamb, fold in the sides and brush the pastry well with melted butter.

6 Roll diagonally to the opposite corner of the sheet. Place join side down on a buttered baking sheet and brush all over with the remaining melted butter. Bake for about 30 minutes or until golden brown.

7 Blend the remaining pears and their juice with the fresh mint. Place the pastry-covered lamb on a large warmed serving plate, garnish with fresh flat leaf parsley and serve immediately with the sauce.

Quiche Lorraine

This classic quiche has some delightful characteristics that are often forgotten in modern recipes: very thin pastry, a really creamy and light, egg-rich filling and smoked bacon.

Serves 4–6

INGREDIENTS

175 g/6 oz/1½ cups plain
    flour, sifted
pinch of salt
150 g/5 oz/10 tbsp unsalted butter,
    at room temperature, diced
3 eggs, plus 3 yolks
6 smoked streaky bacon rashers,
    rind removed
300 ml/½ pint/1¼ cups
    double cream
salt and freshly ground
    black pepper

1 Place the flour, salt, 115 g/4 oz/ ½ cup of the butter and one egg yolk in a food processor and process until blended. Tip out on to a lightly floured surface and bring the mixture together into a ball. Leave to rest for 20 minutes.

COOK'S TIP: To prepare the quiche in advance, bake it for 5–10 minutes less than the time recommended, until just set. Reheat later at 190°C/375°F/ Gas 5 for about 10 minutes.

2 Lightly flour a deep, 20 cm/8 in, round flan tin and place it on a baking sheet. Roll out the pastry and use to line the tin, gently pressing it into the corners. If the pastry breaks up, do not worry: just gently push it into shape. Trim off any overhanging pieces. Chill for 20 minutes. Preheat the oven to 200°C/400°F/Gas 6.

3 Meanwhile, cut the bacon into thin strips and grill until the fat runs. Arrange the bacon in the pastry case. Beat together the cream, the remaining eggs and yolks and seasoning and pour into the pastry case.

4 Bake for 15 minutes, then reduce the heat to 180°C/350°F/Gas 4 and bake for a further 15–20 minutes. When the filling is puffed and golden and the pastry edge crisp, remove from the oven and top with the remaining diced butter. Stand for 5 minutes before serving.

VARIATION: Some versions of this quiche incorporate grated cheese into the filling. Gruyère is very good, although Cheddar can also be used. Simply sprinkle a little cheese over the bacon before adding the cream mixture.

Greek Pies

If you can, use large muffin tins to make these tangy little pies.

Makes 8

INGREDIENTS

175 g/6 oz shortcrust pastry,
 defrosted if frozen
45–60 ml/3–4 tbsp tapenade or sun-dried
 tomato purée
1 large egg
100 g/3¾ oz/scant ½ cup thick
 Greek-style yogurt
90 ml/6 tbsp milk
1 garlic clove, crushed
30 ml/2 tbsp chopped fresh mixed herbs,
 such as thyme, marjoram, basil and parsley
salt and freshly ground black pepper

1 Preheat the oven to 190°C/375°F/
Gas 5. On a lightly floured surface, roll
out the pastry thinly and cut out eight
rounds using a 7.5 cm/3 in cutter.
Line deep patty or muffin tins with
the pastry rounds, then line each with
a small piece of greaseproof paper.

2 Bake for 15 minutes. Remove the
paper and cook for a further 5 minutes
or until crisp and dry. Spread a little
tapenade or tomato purée in each.

3 Whisk together the remaining
ingredients. Spoon into the cases and
bake for 25–30 minutes or until the
filling is just firm and the pastry golden.

Right: Greek Pies (top); Olive Tart

Olive Tart

This delicious tart has a fresh, rich Mediterranean flavour.

Serves 8

INGREDIENTS

375 g/13 oz shortcrust pastry, defrosted if
 frozen and brought to room temperature
3 eggs, beaten
300 ml/½ pint/1¼ cups milk
30 ml/2 tbsp chopped fresh herbs, such as
 parsley, marjoram or basil
6 firm plum tomatoes, sliced
75 g/3 oz ripe Brie cheese, cubed
about 16 black olives, pitted and sliced
salt and freshly ground black pepper

1 Preheat the oven to 190°C/375°F/
Gas 5. Roll out the pastry thinly on a
lightly floured surface. Line a 28 x
18 cm/11 x 7 in, loose-based flan tin,
trimming off any overhanging edges.

2 Line the pastry with greaseproof
paper and baking beans and bake blind
for 15 minutes. Remove the paper and
beans and bake for 5 minutes more
until the base is crisp.

3 Meanwhile, mix together the eggs,
milk, seasoning and herbs. Place the
prepared flan case on a baking sheet,
arrange the tomatoes, cheese and olives
in the bottom of the case, then pour in
the egg mixture. Transfer to the oven
and bake for about 40 minutes until
just firm and turning golden. Slice hot
or cool in the tin, then serve.

Caramelized Onion Tart

Served warm with a mixed leaf salad, this classic and elegant French tart makes a perfect light summer lunch.

Serves 6

INGREDIENTS
75 g/3 oz/⅔ cup plain flour
75 g/3 oz/⅔ cup wholemeal flour
75 g/3 oz/6 tbsp unsalted butter
1 egg yolk

FOR THE FILLING
15 g/½ oz/1 tbsp unsalted butter
15 ml/1 tbsp olive oil
500 g/1¼ lb onions, sliced
large pinch of ground nutmeg
5 ml/1 tsp soft dark
   brown sugar
2 eggs
150 ml/¼ pint/⅔ cup single cream
50 g/2 oz/⅔ cup Gruyère
   cheese, grated
salt and freshly ground
   black pepper

1 Rub together the plain and wholemeal flours and butter until the mixture resembles fine breadcrumbs. Mix in the egg yolk and enough cold water to form a dough.

2 Turn out the dough on to a lightly floured surface and knead gently until smooth. Form into a ball, then wrap in clear film and chill in the fridge for about 30 minutes.

3 Meanwhile, to make the filling, heat the butter and oil in a large, heavy-based frying pan. Cook the onions over a low heat for 30 minutes until very soft and translucent, stirring often. Stir in the nutmeg, sugar and seasoning and cook for a further 5 minutes until the onions are golden and caramelized. Set aside and allow to cool slightly.

4 Preheat the oven to 220°C/425°F/ Gas 7. Lightly grease a loose-based, 35 x 12 cm/14 x 4½ in, fluted flan tin. Roll out the pastry and use to line the prepared tin. Trim the top, then chill for 20 minutes.

5 Prick the pastry base with a fork, then line with greaseproof paper and baking beans and bake blind for 10 minutes until lightly golden. Remove the paper and beans, then spoon the onions into the case.

6 Beat the eggs with the cream, then add the cheese and season to taste with salt and freshly ground black pepper. Pour the mixture over the onions and bake for 30 minutes until set and golden. Serve warm or cold.

Chestnut, Stilton & Ale Pie

This hearty winter dish has a rich gravy and a herb pastry top. The Stilton adds a delicious creaminess but can be omitted if you prefer.

Serves 4

INGREDIENTS
115 g/4 oz/1 cup wholemeal flour
pinch of salt
50 g/2 oz/4 tbsp unsalted butter
  or margarine
15 ml/1 tbsp fresh or 5 ml/1 tsp dried thyme

FOR THE FILLING
30 ml/2 tbsp sunflower oil
2 large onions, chopped
500 g/1¼ lb/8 cups button
  mushrooms, halved
3 carrots, sliced
1 parsnip, cut into thick slices
15 ml/1 tbsp fresh or 5 ml/1 tsp
  dried thyme
2 bay leaves
250 ml/8 fl oz/1 cup pale ale or
  Murphy's Stout
120 ml/4 fl oz/½ cup vegetable stock
5 ml/1 tsp vegetarian Worcestershire sauce
5 ml/1 tsp soft dark brown sugar
350 g/12 oz/3 cups canned chestnuts, halved
30 ml/2 tbsp plain flour
150 g/5 oz/1¼ cups Stilton cheese, cubed
beaten egg or milk, to glaze
salt and freshly ground black pepper

1 Rub together the flour, salt and butter or margarine until the mixture resembles fine breadcrumbs. Add the thyme and enough water to form a soft dough.

2 Turn out the dough on to a floured surface and knead gently for 1 minute until smooth. Wrap in clear film and chill for 30 minutes.

3 To make the filling, heat the oil in a saucepan and fry the onions for 5 minutes until softened. Add the mushrooms and cook for 3 minutes or until just tender. Add the carrots, parsnip and herbs, cover and cook for 3 minutes until slightly softened.

4 Pour in the ale or stout, stock and Worcestershire sauce, then add the sugar and seasoning. Simmer, covered, for 5 minutes, stirring occasionally. Add the chestnuts.

5 Mix the flour to a thin paste with 30 ml/2 tbsp water. Add to the pan and cook, uncovered, for 5 minutes until the sauce thickens, stirring. Stir in the cheese and heat until melted, stirring constantly. Preheat the oven to 220°C/425°F/Gas 7.

6 Roll out the pastry to fit the top of a 1.5 litre/2½ pint/6¼ cup, deep pie dish. Spoon the chestnut mixture into the dish. Dampen the edges of the dish and cover with the pastry.

7 Seal, trim and crimp the edges. Cut a small slit in the top of the pie and use any trimmings to decorate. Brush with egg or milk and bake for 30 minutes until golden. Serve hot.

Goat's Cheese Pastries

These attractive, delicious little pastries are simplicity itself to make.

Serves 4

INGREDIENTS
15 ml/1 tbsp olive oil
450 g/1 lb red onions, sliced
30 ml/2 tbsp fresh or 10 ml/2 tsp
   dried thyme
15 ml/1 tbsp balsamic vinegar
425 g/15 oz ready-rolled puff pastry
115 g/4 oz/½ cup goat's cheese, cubed
1 egg, beaten
salt and freshly ground black pepper
fresh thyme sprigs, to garnish
salad leaves, to serve (optional)

1 Heat the oil in a large, heavy-based frying pan, add the onions and fry over a gentle heat for 10 minutes or until softened, stirring occasionally to prevent them browning.

2 Add the thyme, seasoning and balsamic vinegar and cook for a further 5 minutes. Remove the pan from the heat and leave to cool.

3 Preheat the oven to 220°C/425°F/ Gas 7. Unroll the pastry and, using a 15 cm/6 in plate as a guide, cut four rounds. Place the pastry rounds on a dampened baking sheet. With the point of a knife, score a border 2 cm/¾ in inside the edge of each round.

4 Divide the onions among the pastry rounds and top with the goat's cheese. Brush the edge of each round with beaten egg and bake the pastries for 25–30 minutes until golden. Garnish with fresh thyme sprigs before serving with salad leaves, if you like.

Wild Mushroom Tart

A pastry case packed with well-flavoured mushrooms in a creamy sauce.

Serves 4

INGREDIENTS
350 g/12 oz shortcrust pastry, defrosted
  if frozen
50 g/2 oz/4 tbsp unsalted butter
3 medium onions, sliced
350 g/12 oz/5 cups assorted wild mushrooms
  such as ceps, bay boletus,
  morels, chanterelles, saffron milk-caps,
  oyster, field and Caesar's
  mushrooms, sliced
leaves of 1 fresh thyme
  sprig, chopped
pinch of freshly grated nutmeg
50 ml/2 fl oz/¼ cup full-fat milk
50 ml/2 fl oz/¼ cup single cream
1 egg and 2 egg yolks
salt and freshly ground
  black pepper

1 Preheat the oven 190°C/375°F/
Gas 5 and lightly butter a 23 cm/9 in,
loose-bottomed flan tin. Roll out the
pastry on a lightly floured surface and
line the tin. Chill for 1 hour, then line
with greaseproof paper, fill with baking
beans and bake blind for 25 minutes.
Lift out the paper and beans. Let cool.

2 Melt the butter in a frying pan, add
the onions, cover and cook slowly for
20 minutes. Add the mushrooms and
thyme and cook for 10 minutes more.
Add salt, pepper and nutmeg.

3 Beat the milk and cream in a jug
with the egg and yolks. Place the
mushroom in the flan case and then
pour over the egg mixture. Bake for
15–20 minutes until firm. Serve warm.

Cheese & Spinach Flan

This spectacular flan makes an excellent addition to a festive buffet party, and is not as complicated as it looks.

Serves 8

INGREDIENTS
115 g/4 oz/½ cup butter
225 g/8 oz/2 cups plain flour
2.5 ml/½ tsp English mustard powder
2.5 ml/½ tsp paprika
large pinch of salt
115 g/4 oz/1 cup Cheddar cheese,
    finely grated
45–60 ml/3–4 tbsp cold water
beaten egg, to glaze

FOR THE FILLING
450 g/1 lb frozen spinach, thawed
1 onion, chopped
pinch of freshly grated nutmeg
225 g/8 oz/1 cup cottage cheese
2 large eggs
50 g/2 oz/⅔ cup Parmesan cheese, grated
150 ml/¼ pint/⅔ cup single cream
salt and freshly ground black pepper

1 Mix the flour with the mustard, paprika and salt, and rub in the butter until it resembles fine breadcrumbs. Add the cheese and bind to a dough with the cold water. Knead until smooth, form into a ball and chill for 30 minutes.

> COOK'S TIP: This flan freezes well and can be reheated, making it ideal for entertaining.

2 To make the filling, put the spinach and onion in a pan, cover and cook slowly for five minutes. Uncover and increase the heat to drive off any water. Transfer to a bowl to cool. Add the remaining filling ingredients.

3 Preheat the oven to 200°C/400°F/ Gas 6. Put a baking sheet in the oven to heat. Reserve one-third of the pastry for the lid. On a lightly floured surface, roll out the remaining pastry and use it to line a 23 cm/9 in, loose-based flan tin. Make a narrow lip around the top edge. Remove the excess pastry with a rolling pin. Spoon the filling into the flan case.

4 Roll out the reserved pastry and cut it firmly with a lattice pastry cutter. Carefully open the lattice. With the help of a rolling pin, lay it over the flan.

5 Brush the joins in the pastry with the beaten egg glaze. Press the edges together with your fingertips and trim off the excess pastry.

6 Alternatively, cut the pastry into 1 cm/½ in strips and arrange them in a lattice on top of the flan, brushing the joins with egg and pressing well together to seal.

7 Brush the pastry lattice with egg and bake on the baking sheet for 35–40 minutes or until golden brown. Serve hot or cold.

Vegetable Tarte Tatin

This upside-down tart, which combines Mediterranean vegetables with a medley of rice, garlic, onions and olives, makes a great starter.

Serves 4 as a starter

INGREDIENTS
30 ml/2 tbsp sunflower oil
about 25 ml/1½ tbsp olive oil
1 aubergine, sliced lengthways
1 large red pepper, seeded and cut into
    long strips
5 tomatoes
2 red shallots, finely chopped
1–2 garlic cloves, crushed
150 ml/¼ pint/⅔ cup white wine
10 ml/2 tsp chopped fresh basil
225 g/8 oz/1⅓ cups cooked white or brown
    long grain rice
40 g/1½ oz/⅔ cup pitted black
    olives, chopped
350 g/12 oz puff pastry, defrosted if frozen
freshly ground black pepper
salad leaves, to serve

1 Preheat the oven to 190°C/375°F/ Gas 5. Heat the sunflower oil with 15 ml/1 tbsp of the olive oil in a frying pan and fry the aubergine slices for 4–5 minutes on each side until golden brown. Lift out and drain on kitchen paper.

2 Add the pepper strips to the oil remaining in the pan, turning them to coat. Cover the pan and sweat the peppers over a moderately high heat for 5–6 minutes, stirring occasionally, until they are soft and flecked with brown.

3 Slice two of the tomatoes and set them aside. Plunge the remaining tomatoes into boiling water for 20-30 seconds, then peel them, cut them into quarters and discard the core and seeds. Chop the flesh roughly.

4 Heat the remaining oil in the frying pan and fry the shallots and garlic for 3–4 minutes until softened. Add the chopped tomatoes and cook for a few minutes until softened. Stir in the wine and basil, with black pepper to taste. Bring to the boil, then remove from the heat and stir in the cooked rice and black olives.

5 Arrange the tomato slices, aubergine slices and peppers in a single layer over the bottom of a heavy, 30 cm/12 in, shallow ovenproof dish or tin. Spread the rice mixture on top.

VARIATION: You could use sliced courgettes instead of aubergines.

6 Roll out the pastry to a circle slightly larger than the diameter of the dish or tin and place on top of the rice, tucking the overlap down inside the edge.

7 Bake for 25–30 minutes until the pastry is golden and risen. Cool slightly, then invert the tart on to a large, warmed serving plate. Serve in slices, with salad leaves.

French Apple Tart

This glorious tart makes a truly indulgent dessert. For an early morning treat, try a slice for breakfast with a cup of strong black coffee.

Serves 8

INGREDIENTS
350 g/12 oz sweet shortcrust pastry,
   defrosted if frozen
whipped cream, to serve

FOR THE FILLING
115 g/4 oz/½ cup butter, softened
115 g/4 oz/½ cup caster sugar
2 large eggs, beaten
115 g/4 oz/1 cup ground almonds
25 g/1 oz/¼ cup plain flour

FOR THE TOPPING
3 Braeburn apples
60 ml/4 tbsp apricot jam
15 ml/1 tbsp water

1 Preheat the oven to 190°C/375°F/ Gas 5. Place a baking sheet in the oven to heat. Roll out the pastry on a lightly floured surface and line a 23 cm/9 in, fluted flan tin.

2 To make the filling, beat all the ingredients together until light and fluffy. Spoon into the pastry case and level the surface.

VARIATION: A redcurrant glaze would also look good on this tart. Warm redcurrant jelly with a little lemon juice. Brush over the apples.

3 To make the topping, peel and core the apples and cut in half. Place each half, cut side down, on a board. Using a sharp, fine knife, slice the apples thinly, keeping the shape, then press down lightly to fan each apple half in a row.

4 Using a palette knife, carefully transfer each row of apple slices to the tart, arranging them on top of the filling so that they resemble the spokes of a wheel. You may need to overlap the slices in the middle slightly to fit. Press the slices down well into the filling to secure.

5 Warm the apricot jam with the water, then press the mixture through a sieve into a small bowl. Brush half the jam glaze over the apples. Place the tin on the baking sheet and bake the tart for 35 minutes or until the pastry is golden and the apples have started to singe slightly.

6 Rewarm the remaining jam glaze and brush it over the apples. Let the tart cool slightly before serving with cream.

43

Red Grape & Cheese Tartlets

Fruit and cheese form a natural combination in this simple recipe. Look out for red grapes, which tend to be sweeter than black grapes.

Makes 6

INGREDIENTS
350 g/12 oz sweet shortcrust pastry, defrosted if frozen
225 g/8 oz/1 cup curd cheese
150 ml/¼ pint/⅔ cup double cream
2.5 ml/½ tsp pure vanilla essence
30 ml/2 tbsp icing sugar
200 g/7 oz/2 cups red grapes, halved, seeded if necessary
60 ml/4 tbsp apricot conserve
15 ml/1 tbsp water

1 Preheat the oven to 200°C/400°F/Gas 6. On a lightly floured surface, roll out the pastry and use to line six deep, 9 cm/3½ in, fluted individual tartlet tins, pressing well into the sides. Trim off any excess pastry with a knife or scissors. Prick the bases with a fork and line with greaseproof paper and baking beans.

2 Bake for 10 minutes, remove the paper and beans, then return the cases to the oven for 5 minutes until golden and fully cooked. Remove from the tins and cool on a wire rack.

3 Beat the curd cheese, double cream, vanilla essence and icing sugar in a bowl. Divide the mixture among the pastry cases. Smooth the surface and arrange the halved grapes on top.

4 Sieve the apricot conserve into a pan. Add the water and heat, stirring, until smooth. Spoon over the grapes. Cool, then chill before serving.

VARIATIONS: Use cranberry jelly or redcurrant jelly for the glaze. There is no need to sieve. Also vary the fruit topping: try blackberries, blueberries, raspberries, strawberries, kiwi fruit, banana or pineapple slices.

Classic Lemon Tart

The yellower the egg yolks, the better the colour of this scrumptious tart.

Serves 8

INGREDIENTS

150 g/5 oz/1¼ cups plain flour, sifted
50 g/2 oz/½ cup hazelnuts, toasted and
    finely ground
175 g/6 oz/scant 1 cup caster sugar
115 g/4 oz/½ cup unsalted butter, softened
4 eggs
finely grated rind of 2 lemons and at least
    175 ml/6 fl oz/¾ cup lemon juice
150 ml/¼ pint/⅔ cup double cream

1 Mix together the flour, nuts and 25 g/1 oz/2 tbsp of the sugar. Gently work in the butter and, if necessary, 15–30 ml/1–2 tbsp cold water to make a soft dough. Chill the dough for 10 minutes.

2 Roll out the dough and use to line a 20 cm/8 in, loose-based flan tin. If you find it too difficult to roll out, push the pastry into the flan tin. Chill for about 20 minutes. Preheat the oven to 200°C/400°F/Gas 6.

3 Line the pastry case with greaseproof paper, fill with baking beans and bake for 15 minutes. Remove the paper and beans and cook for a further 5–10 minutes until the base is crisp.

4 Beat the eggs, lemon rind and juice, the cream and remaining sugar, until well blended. Pour into the pastry case. Bake for about 30 minutes until just set. Serve warm or cold.

Orange Curd Tarts

These English tarts combine a creamy filling with a hint of Cointreau.

Makes 6

INGREDIENTS
175 g/6 oz/1½ cups plain flour
40 g/1½ oz/3 tbsp block margarine, diced
40 g/1½ oz/3 tbsp white cooking fat, diced
30 ml/2 tbsp caster sugar
1 medium egg yolk
2.5 ml/½ tsp freshly grated nutmeg
orange segments and thinly pared orange
    rind, to decorate

FOR THE FILLING
25 g/1 oz/2 tbsp butter, melted
50 g/2 oz/¼ cup caster sugar
1 egg
175 g/6 oz/¾ cup curd cheese
30 ml/2 tbsp double cream
50 g/2 oz/¼ cup currants
15 ml/1 tbsp grated lemon rind
15 ml/1 tbsp grated orange rind
15 ml/1 tbsp Cointreau

1 Sift the flour into a large mixing bowl and rub in the margarine and fat until the mixture resembles fine breadcrumbs. Stir in the sugar and egg yolk and add enough cold water to make a firm dough. Chill in the fridge for 30 minutes.

2 Preheat the oven to 190°C/375°F/ Gas 5. Roll out the dough on a lightly floured surface and line six 10 cm/ 4 in, fluted flan tins.

3 To make the filling, combine the melted butter, sugar, egg, curd cheese, cream, currants, grated lemon and orange rind and Cointreau in a bowl. Mix well. Spoon into the pastry cases, sprinkle over the nutmeg and bake for 30–35 minutes until golden. Serve decorated with orange segments and thinly pared rind.

Blueberry Pie

It is worth taking the time to decorate this beautiful pie, which tastes as good as it looks.

Serves 8

INGREDIENTS
225 g/8 oz/2 cups flour
2.5 ml/½ tsp salt
115 g/4 oz/½ cup chilled butter,
    cut into pieces
40 g/1½ oz/3 tbsp chilled white cooking fat,
    cut into pieces
75–90 ml/5–6 tbsp iced water
1 egg beaten with 15 ml/1 tbsp water,
    to glaze

FOR THE FILLING
450 g/1 lb/4 cups blueberries
90 g/3½ oz/½ cup sugar
45 ml/3 tbsp cornflour
30 ml/2 tbsp lemon juice
25 g/1 oz/2 tbsp butter, diced

1 Sift the flour and salt into a bowl. Add the butter and fat and cut in with a pastry blender until the mixture resembles coarse crumbs. With a fork, stir in just enough iced water to bind the dough together. Form into two equal balls and place in the fridge to chill for 20 minutes.

2 On a lightly floured surface, roll out one dough ball about 3 mm/⅛ in thick. Transfer to a 23 cm/9 in pie tin and trim to leave a 1 cm/½ in overhang. Brush the bottom with egg glaze.

3 To make the filling, mix together all ingredients except a few of the blueberries and the butter. Spoon the mixture into the pastry case and dot with the butter. Brush the edge of the pastry with egg glaze.

4 Preheat the oven to 220°C/425°F/ Gas 7. Place a baking sheet on the centre shelf to heat.

5 Roll out the remaining dough on a baking sheet lined with greaseproof paper. With a serrated pastry wheel, cut out 24 thin strips of dough. Roll out the trimmings to make leaf shapes. Mark veins in the leaves with a knife.

6 Weave the strips in a close lattice, then transfer to the pie using the greaseproof paper. Press the edges to seal and trim. Arrange the dough leaves around the rim. Brush with egg glaze.

7 Bake for 10 minutes. Reduce the heat to 180°C/350°F/Gas 4 and bake for 40–45 minutes more until the pastry is golden. Decorate with the reserved blueberries and serve.

49

Filo-topped Apple Pie

With its scrunchy filo topping and minimal butter, this makes a really light dessert: a good choice for apple-pie addicts watching their fat intake.

Serves 6

INGREDIENTS
900 g/2 lb Bramley or other
  cooking apples
75 g/3 oz/scant ½ cup caster sugar
grated rind of 1 lemon
15 ml/1 tbsp lemon juice
75 g/3 oz/½ cup sultanas
2.5 ml/½ tsp ground cinnamon
4 large sheets filo pastry, defrosted
  if frozen
25 g/1 oz/2 tbsp butter, melted
icing sugar, for dusting
custard or cream,
  to serve

1 Peel, core and dice the apples. Place them in a saucepan with the caster sugar and lemon rind. Drizzle the lemon juice over.

2 Bring the apple mixture to the boil, stir well, then cook for 5 minutes or until the apples have softened.

3 Stir in the sultanas and cinnamon. Spoon the mixture into a 1.2 litre/ 2 pint/5 cup pie dish and level the top. Allow to cool.

4 Preheat the oven to 180°C/350°F/ Gas 4. Place a pie funnel in the centre of the fruit. Brush each sheet of filo with melted butter. Scrunch up loosely and place on top of the fruit to cover it completely.

5 Bake for 20–30 minutes until the filo pastry is golden. Dust the apple pie with icing sugar before serving with custard or cream.

VARIATION: To make filo crackers, cut the buttered filo into 20 cm/8 in wide strips. Spoon a little of the apple filling along one edge of each strip, leaving the sides clear. Roll up and twist the ends to make a cracker. Brush with more melted butter and bake in the oven for 20 minutes.

Mango Pie

This recipe comes straight from the Caribbean and captures all its sunshine flavours. For the tastiest pie, be sure the mangoes are ripe.

Serves 6

INGREDIENTS
175 g/6 oz/1½ cups plain flour
pinch of salt
75 g/3 oz/6 tbsp chilled unsalted
   butter, diced
25 g/1 oz/2 tbsp chilled white vegetable
   fat, diced
15 ml/1 tbsp caster sugar, plus extra
   for sprinkling
about 45 ml/3 tbsp cold water
beaten egg, to glaze
vanilla ice cream, to serve

FOR THE FILLING
2 ripe mangoes
45 ml/3 tbsp lime juice
115 g/4 oz/generous ½ cup caster sugar
15 ml/1 tbsp arrowroot mixed to a thin paste
   with 15 ml/1 tbsp water

1 Sift the flour and salt into a large mixing bowl. Rub in the butter and fat until the mixture resembles fine breadcrumbs, then stir in the caster sugar. Add just enough of the cold water to make a dough.

2 Knead the pastry lightly on a lightly floured surface, then roll out two-thirds to line a 18 cm/ 7 in pie dish. Chill the pastry case together with the remaining pastry for 30 minutes.

3 Meanwhile, to make the filling, peel the mangoes and slice the flesh off the stone. Reserve half the sliced mango, and coarsely chop the rest.

4 Place the chopped mango in a saucepan with the lime juice and sugar. Cover and cook for 10 minutes or until soft. Pour in the arrowroot paste and cook, stirring all the time, until thickened. Set the filling aside to cool.

5 Preheat the oven to 190°C/375°F/ Gas 5. Pour the cooled sauce into the chilled pastry case and top with all the reserved mango slices. Roll out the remaining pastry to make a lid.

6 Dampen the rim of the pastry case and add the pastry lid. Crimp the edges to seal, then cut a cross in the centre to allow the steam to escape.

7 Glaze the pastry with the beaten egg and sprinkle lightly with caster sugar. Bake for 35–40 minutes until the pastry is golden brown. Cool slightly on a wire rack. Serve warm with vanilla ice cream.

Italian Chocolate Ricotta Pie

This delectable pie has chocolate in both pastry and filling. It travels well and is perfect for picnics.

Serves 6

INGREDIENTS
225 g/8 oz/2 cups plain flour
30 ml/2 tbsp cocoa powder
60 ml/4 tbsp caster sugar
115 g/4 oz/½ cup unsalted butter
60 ml/4 tbsp dry sherry
whipped cream, to serve

FOR THE FILLING
2 egg yolks
115 g/4 oz/generous ½ cup
   caster sugar
500 g/1¼ lb/2½ cups ricotta cheese
finely grated rind of 1 lemon
90 ml/6 tbsp dark chocolate chips
75 ml/5 tbsp chopped
   mixed peel
45 ml/3 tbsp chopped angelica

1 Preheat the oven to 200°C/400°F/ Gas 6. Sift the flour and cocoa into a bowl, then stir in the sugar. Rub in the butter until the mixture resembles breadcrumbs, then work in the sherry, using your fingertips, until the mixture binds to a firm dough.

2 Roll out three-quarters of the pastry on a lightly floured surface and use it to line a 24 cm/9½ in, loose-based flan tin.

3 To make the filling, beat the egg yolks and sugar in a bowl, then beat in the ricotta cheese to mix thoroughly. Stir in the lemon rind, chocolate chips, mixed peel and angelica.

4 Scrape the ricotta mixture into the pastry case and level the surface. Roll out the remaining pastry and cut into strips, then arrange these in a lattice over the pie.

VARIATION: Instead of sherry you could use brandy or Amaretto.

5 Bake for 15 minutes, then lower the heat to 180°C/350°F/Gas 4 and cook for a further 30–35 minutes until the pastry is golden brown and the filling is firm. Cool in the tin. Serve with whipped cream.

COOK'S TIP: This pie is best served at room temperature, so if you make it in advance, chill it when cool, then bring to room temperature for about 30 minutes before serving.

Chocolate Truffle Tart

Almost any type of liqueur can be substituted for brandy in this recipe.

Serves 12

INGREDIENTS
150 g/5 oz/1¼ cups plain flour
25 g/1 oz/¼ cup unsweetened cocoa powder
50 g/2 oz/¼ cup caster sugar
2.5 ml/½ tsp salt
115 g/4 oz/½ cup chilled unsalted butter,
   in pieces
1 egg yolk
15–30 ml/1–2 tbsp iced water
25 g/1 oz fine-quality white or milk
   chocolate, melted
whipped cream, to serve (optional)

FOR THE TRUFFLE FILLING
335 ml/11 fl oz/1⅓ cups double cream
350 g/12 oz couverture or fine-quality plain
   chocolate, chopped
50 g/2 oz/4 tbsp unsalted butter, in pieces
30 ml/2 tbsp brandy or other liqueur

1 Sift the flour and cocoa into a bowl. In a food processor fitted with metal blade, process the flour mixture, sugar and salt to blend. Add the butter and process for 15–20 seconds until the mixture resembles coarse breadcrumbs.

2 In a bowl, lightly beat the yolk with the water. Add to the flour mixture and, using the pulse action, process to a dough. Turn out on to clear film, use to help shape the dough into a flat disc and wrap tightly. Chill for 1–2 hours until firm.

3 Lightly grease a 23 cm/9 in, loose-based tart tin. Soften the dough for 5–10 minutes, then roll out between sheets of waxed paper or clear film to a 28 cm/11 in round, about 5 mm/ ¼ in thick. Peel off the top sheet and invert into the tin. Remove the bottom sheet. Ease the dough on to the base and sides of the tin. Prick the base and chill for 1 hour.

4 Preheat the oven to 180°C/350°F/ Gas 4. Line the pastry with greaseproof paper and fill with beans. Bake for 5–7 minutes, then lift out the paper and beans and bake for 5–7 minutes more until just set. (The pastry may look underdone on the bottom, but it will dry out.) Cool on a wire rack.

5 For the truffle filling bring the double cream to the boil in a pan over medium heat. Remove from the heat and stir in the couverture or plain chocolate until melted. Stir in the butter and liqueur. Strain evenly into the pastry, but avoid touching.

6 Spoon the melted chocolate into a paper cone and cut a tip about 5 mm/ ¼ in in diameter. Drop rounds of chocolate over the surface of the tart and gently draw the point of a skewer or cocktail stick through the chocolate to produce a marbled effect. Chill for 2–3 hours until set. Allow the tart to soften slightly at room temperature for about 30 minutes before serving with whipped cream, if liked.

Mississippi Mud Pie

This open-topped pie has three layers of "mud": dark chocolate, golden, rum-flavoured custard and whipped cream – sheer ecstasy!

Serves 6–8

INGREDIENTS
250 g/9 oz/2¼ cups plain flour
150 g/5 oz/10 tbsp unsalted butter
2 egg yolks
15–30 ml/1–2 tbsp iced water

FOR THE FILLING
3 eggs, separated
20 ml/4 tsp cornflour
75 g/3 oz/scant ½ cup golden
   caster sugar
400 ml/14 fl oz/1⅔ cups milk
150 g/5 oz plain chocolate, broken
   into squares
5 ml/1 tsp pure vanilla essence
1 sachet powdered gelatine
45 ml/3 tbsp water
30 ml/2 tsp dark rum

FOR THE TOPPING
175 ml/6 fl oz/¾ cup double or
   whipping cream
chocolate curls

1 Sift the flour into a large bowl and rub in the butter until the mixture resembles coarse breadcrumbs. Stir in the egg yolks with just enough iced water to bind the mixture to a soft pliable dough. Roll out on a lightly floured surface and line a deep, 23 cm/9 in flan tin. Chill for about 30 minutes.

2 Preheat the oven to 190°C/375°F/ Gas 5. Prick the pastry case all over with a fork, cover with greaseproof paper weighed down with baking beans and bake blind for 10 minutes. Remove the baking beans and paper, return to the oven and bake for a further 10 minutes until the pastry is crisp and golden. Cool in the tin.

3 To make the filling, mix the egg yolks, cornflour and 30 ml/2 tbsp of the sugar in a bowl. Heat the milk in a saucepan until almost boiling, then beat into the egg mixture. Return to the clean pan and stir over a low heat until the custard has thickened and is smooth. Pour half the custard into a heatproof bowl.

4 Melt the chocolate in a heatproof bowl over hot water, then stir into the custard in the bowl, with the vanilla essence. Spread in the pastry case, cover closely to prevent the formation of a skin, cool, then chill until set.

5 Sprinkle the gelatine over the water in a small bowl, leave until spongy, then place over simmering water until all the gelatine has dissolved. Stir into the remaining custard, with the rum. Whisk the egg whites in a clean, grease-free bowl until stiff peaks form, whisk in the remaining sugar, then fold quickly into the custard before it sets.

6 Spoon the mixture over the chocolate custard to cover completely. Chill until set, then remove the pie from the tin and place on a large serving plate.

7 Spread whipped cream over the top, sprinkle with the chocolate curls and serve.

Chocolate Pecan Pie

If you thought pecan pie could not be improved upon, just try this
gorgeous chocolate version with its rich orange crust.

Serves 6

INGREDiENTS
200 g/7 oz/1¾ cups plain flour
65 g/2½ oz/5 tbsp caster sugar
90 g/3⅓ oz/7 tbsp unsalted
   butter, softened
1 egg, beaten
finely grated rind of 1 orange

FOR THE FILLING
200 g/7 oz/generous ½ cup
   golden syrup
45 ml/3 tbsp soft light
   muscovado sugar
150 g/5 oz plain chocolate,
   broken into squares
50 g/2 oz/4 tbsp butter
3 eggs, beaten
5 ml/1 tsp pure vanilla essence
175 g/6 oz/1½ cups pecan nuts

1 Sift the flour into a bowl and stir in
the sugar. Work in the butter evenly
with the fingertips until combined to
form coarse crumbs.

2 Beat the egg and orange rind in
another bowl, then stir into the flour
mixture to make a firm dough. Add a
little water if the mixture is too dry.

3 Roll out the pastry on a lightly
floured surface and use to line a deep,
20 cm/8 in, loose-based flan tin. Chill
for 30 minutes.

4 Preheat the oven to 180°C/350°F/
Gas 4. To make the filling, mix the
golden syrup, sugar, chocolate and
butter in a small saucepan. Heat gently,
stirring, until melted.

VARIATIONS: Make individual
tartlets if you prefer – just use six
10 cm/4 in flan tins and bake at
the same temperature for about
30 minutes. Walnuts or almonds
can be used instead of pecan nuts.

5 Remove the chocolate mixture from the heat and beat in the eggs and vanilla essence. Sprinkle the pecan nuts into the pastry case and carefully pour over the chocolate mixture.

6 Place on a baking sheet and bake for 50 minutes–1 hour or until set. Cool in the tin before serving.

Chocolate Pine Nut Tart

Lemon rind could be used instead of orange and a combination of white and plain chocolate substituted for all plain.

Serves 8

INGREDIENTS
200 g/7½ oz/scant 2 cups plain flour
50 g/2 oz/¼ cup caster sugar
pinch of salt
grated rind of ½ orange
115 g/4 oz/½ cup unsalted butter, cut into
    small pieces
3 egg yolks, lightly beaten
15–30 ml/1–2 tbsp iced water

FOR THE FILLING
2 eggs
40 g/1½ oz/3 tbsp caster sugar
grated rind of 1 orange
15 ml/1 tbsp orange-flavour liqueur
250 ml/8 fl oz/1 cup whipping cream
115 g/4 oz plain chocolate, chopped
75 g/3 oz/¾ cup pine nuts, toasted

FOR THE DECORATION
1 orange
50 g/2 oz/¼ cup granulated sugar
120 ml/4 fl oz/½ cup water

1 In a food processor, process the flour, sugar, salt and orange rind to blend. Add the butter and process for 20–30 seconds until it resembles coarse crumbs. Add the yolks and pulse until it begins to combine; do not allow to form a ball. If it is dry, add 15–30 ml/ 1–2 tbsp iced water, little by little, just until it holds.

2 Turn on to a lightly floured surface. Knead gently until blended. Shape into a disc and wrap in clear film. Chill for 2–3 hours or overnight.

3 Lightly butter a 23 cm/9 in, loose-based tart tin. Soften the dough for 5–10 minutes. On a well-floured surface, roll out the dough to a 28 cm/ 11 in round, about 3 mm/⅛ in thick and line the tin.

4 Roll a rolling pin over the edge to cut off excess dough. Now press the thicker top edge against the side of the tin to form a rim slightly higher than the tin. Prick the base with a fork. Chill for 1 hour. Preheat the oven to 200°C/400°F/Gas 6.

5 Line the pastry with greaseproof paper and baking beans and bake for 5 minutes. Lift out the paper and beans and bake for 5 more minutes until set. Cool slightly on a rack. Lower the heat to 180°C/350°F/Gas 4.

6 To make the filling, beat the eggs, sugar, rind and liqueur together. Blend in the cream. Sprinkle the chocolate, and pine nuts evenly over the bottom of the pastry. Place the tin on a baking sheet and gently pour the egg mixture into the case. Bake for 20–30 minutes until the pastry is golden and the custard set. Cool slightly then transfer the tart to a wire rack.

7 To make the decoration, remove thin strips of orange rind and cut into julienne strips. Boil for 5–8 minutes with the sugar and water, until the syrup is thickened, then stir in 15 ml/ 1 tbsp cold water to halt the cooking.

8 Carefully brush the tart with the orange-sugar syrup and arrange julienne orange strips over the top.

This edition is published by Southwater

Southwater is an imprint of
Anness Publishing Ltd
Hermes House
88-89 Blackfriars Road,
London SE1 8HA
tel. 020 7401 2077
fax 020 7633 9499

Distributed in the UK by
The Manning Partnership
251–253 London Road East
Batheaston
Bath BA1 7RL
tel. 01225 852 727
fax 01225 852 852

Distributed in the USA by
Anness Publishing Inc.
27 West 20th Street
Suite 504, New York NY 10011
tel. 212 807 6739
fax 212 807 6813

Distributed in Australia by
Sandstone Publishing
Unit 1, 360 Norton Street, Leichhardt
New South Wales 2040
tel. 02 9560 7888
fax 02 9560 7488

1 3 5 7 9 10 8 6 4 2

Publisher: Joanna Lorenz
Editor: Valerie Ferguson
Series Designer: Bobbie Colgate Stone
Designer: Andrew Heath
Production Controller: Joanna King

Recipes contributed by: Catherine Atkinson,
Alex Barker, Carla Capalbo, Frances Cleary,
Trish Davies, Matthew Drennan, Christine France,
Nicola Graimes, Judy Jackson, Sue Maggs,
Sally Mansfield, Maggie Mayhew,
Christine McFadden, Norma Miller,
Katherine Richmond, Steven Wheeler,
Elizabeth Wolf-Cohen.

Photography: William Adams-Lingwood,
Karl Adamson, Edward Allwright, Steve Baxter,
James Duncan, John Freeman, Ian Garlick,
Michelle Garrett, Amanda Heywood,
David Jordan, Don Last, Steve Moss,
Thomas Odulate, Sam Stowell.

Notes:
For all recipes, quantities are given in both metric and imperial measures and, where appropriate, measures are also given in standard cups and spoons.
Follow one set, but not a mixture, because they are not interchangeable.

Standard spoon and cup measures are level.

1 tsp = 5 ml   1 tbsp = 15 ml

1 cup = 250 ml/8 fl oz

Australian standard tablespoons are 20 ml.
Australian readers should use 3 tsp in place of 1 tbsp for measuring small quantities of gelatine, cornflour, salt etc.

Medium eggs are used unless otherwise stated.